RANDOLPH WRIGHT

Confessions of a
BLACK
GAY
MAN

LIFE, LUST, AND
CONQUERING HATE

"To my mother, for always telling me I have a story to write."

CONTENTS

CHAPTER 1. A LITTLE BOY

Growing up, everyone knew I was queer. They knew I was different. I had a very high voice, and apparently, it was more "girly" than the girls, and for that reason, I got picked on and bullied when I was in pre-school, but my elder sister would always swoop in like a wonder woman and protect me. She always protected me. I remember going to church, waiting at the bus stop, and being at any other family or friend gatherings—all the other kids and, sometimes, the adults would always make it very obvious of my feminine qualities: "Why does he talk like that?" "Why is he holding his hands like that?" "Why does he walk like that?" I never thought about how I carried myself until they made fun of me, and as I got older, I knew I had to find a way to hide these characteristics about myself that were obviously a problem.

Growing up, we bounced between Forrest City and Jonesboro Arkansas, and at that time, all my critics were people who looked like me—Black. It was from my community, from my culture, and from my family that I experienced a mild form of hate and non-acceptance, and I feel this eventually had a crucial part in the type of people I would eventually have a strong attraction to... I knew I was gay when I was in kindergarten. And I know most people would be like, that's impossible, you were a child, you didn't know any better. But I did. To this day, I tell my sister these kids are a lot smarter than we think. We grew up watching a lot of stuff we had no business watching, and I remember being so fascinated, excited, and just happy to see any type of male-on-male relationships on TV. I knew I was "supposed" to like girls but I didn't. All throughout grade school, I would make it a point to let everyone know that I like the most pretty, most popular girl... It was a big lie. Two Black girls, in particular, will always stand out to me, because as much as I wanted to use them as a cover for their popularity and beauty, they absolutely hated me and treated me like shit—called me ugly, said I had big lips, and would always say I was just lame.

I was being rejected by my own people on so many levels, and deep down, it hurt. I remember a very close and stronghold family member saying, "they need to put all them gay people in a big bag and burn them." I also heard my other family members express their disgust for "faggots," and my daddy never showed me the love he did for my sister, and I knew it was because he knew I was "different." He would also antagonize me by sometimes talking to me in a "sweet, sissified way" from time to time, and I knew exactly what he was doing, and I absolutely despised him for it. The thing is he would never do it in front of my mother or sister. I sometimes think he was wondering if I would be attracted to it, like I was going to give him some type of confirmation by somehow being lured into expressing myself in some way that gave him the "AHA! Yo little ass is gay!" moment he was seeking. But like I said, I despised it, and I'd always look at him like he was fucking crazy when he did it. But I must confess that even though I was dealing with all this rejection and subtle resentment was being created deep in my subconscious, my family still loved me and I loved them...

CHAPTER 2. FRIENDS

Even though my own culture gave me the hardest time, believe it or not, my best friend growing up was Black. My extremely loving and hardworking mother was determined to get us into a house, and she did, and in this new neighborhood is where I met Deon. He was slightly older than me, and he also had a very strong, caring, and hardworking Black mother. Deon treated me with nothing but respect when we first met. He didn't judge me; he just saw me as another kid at the time. We played video games, basketball, liked the same music, and even went to church where I was once again scrutinized by my queer characteristics, but like a big brother, Deon stood up for me and would always take it one step further and challenge them to games of basketball because he knew how good I was and that there was nothing sissy about how I played. We'd always win and that made them really want to fight me, but Deon was like an elder brother to me and protected me just like my sister did.

I was above average height for my age growing up and very athletic; after all my All-Star mama was legitimately a

Basketball All Star in both high school and college. The people in Jonesboro knew that, and this gave me the opportunity to spend a lot of time with kids outside my race, mainly other White kids, who I played YMCA sports, AAU basketball, and other extracurricular activities with.

The key thing that I realized about the White kids was they didn't bully me. They didn't criticize me about my queerness, but more so just ignored me or just never spoke to me. If they didn't do that, they were extremely nice to me, and I being the unique critical thinker at such a young age was fascinated by it; I took notice to it, and I feel it planted a seed of preference that would influence my future relationships as I got older. I also took notice to their lifestyles. Everything they had was so much better. Big houses, nice cars, all the snacks and juices, and their parents would often treat me better than their own kids, so much so that I sensed the jealousy from time to time when I would come around, but their kids would never take it out on me. I just noticed they'd get quiet, and borderline seem a bit sad, and then in effort to challenge their parents' kindness, they would try to one up them. I remember one time one of my White friends snuck me in his parents' room and showed me his dad's Superbowl Ring. I didn't really realize the significance of it until I got older; *damn, his dad won the Superbowl!*

I was so intrigued by these White folks because not only did I know I was gay at a young age, but I was also fully aware of the racial tension that stains America till this very day. We grew up watching a lot of documentaries, movies, and shows that highlighted the unimaginable racism this country was built on. We even experienced a few incidents where the KKK (Ku Klux Klan) went around hanging posters in my parents' hometown of Forrest City, telling Black folks "BEWARE!" And of course, we had those moments of being followed around in department stores, bad service, and a variety of other mistreatments that blatantly fell under the umbrella of racism... So, from a very early age, I had to learn how to process all this hate.

I must confess I was confused thinking certain people from my own culture have mistreated me, and certain people who come from a culture of evil doings have treated me with kindness. I was also afraid of what the future meant for me to grow up Black and gay in America.

CHAPTER 3. HIDING

I knew I was different. I knew I had to hide this "flaw." Me realizing I was gay, I needed to hide it. So what did I do? I acted out. Mainly by stealing. I was a little thief. I would steal from everybody—Family, friends, the store, school. If there was something I saw and I wanted it and the opportunity presented itself for me to steal it, I was going for it. I got caught a few times and my mama beat my ass. But I didn't care. I was hoping it would take their mind off me thinking I might be gay, but they probably just thought we have a little gay thief on our hands. A gay bandit. It didn't stop there... Growing up, I spent a lot of time with my sister and cousin Kayla. Kayla was always in grown folks' business, and when they would leave us at the house alone, she would show us the "tapes." The "tapes" were porn. Like I said before, we grew up watching a lot of stuff we had no business watching. Our minds were blown watching these people have sex; we would always question "what's that white stuff coming out his thang????" I even went as far as making a move on my cousin Kayla to try and prove to myself

I didn't like boys. My sister caught us under the bed with just our underwear on and ran and told our granny, and we both got our ass beat. I still get embarrassed thinking about that.

I made it a point to really focus on the things that people would make fun of me the most. Mainly how I would walk and hold my hands. My voice was very high for a while, and there wasn't too much I could do about that. Basketball ended up being a huge safety net for me. I loved to play, I loved to practice, and I was better than the majority of the kids who were making fun of me. The bigger kids were the only ones who could actually stop me, and I had moments where I would show them up, and they'd get mad and start to rough me up on the court by playing rough, knocking me down, calling me a sissy, faggot… I didn't care. It just made me feel good that I knew this little gay boy was making them mad by beating them in basketball. Basketball was my number one cover. I knew how good my mom was, and I wanted to be a star like her; practicing basketball was also the one thing I knew my dad enjoyed with me and my sister, and it possibly gave him hope of me not being gay.

As I grew older, I made it a point to really put a focus on school and basketball. So much so that I had developed a solid reputation at eleven years old as a hooper to watch, that it was doing a good job of hiding who I was. I had gotten used to my environment. I learned how to stand up for myself, and I wasn't afraid to fight. Rap music was taking over and I saw that as another avenue for me to hide and I did. I would learn songs and amaze people by giving full-out performances on road trips or anytime I had the chance. I must confess, anything I could do that would take the edge off people questioning my sexuality and that I thought was cool, I would use it to hide; unfortunately, it was a lot of negative stereotypical actions I'd portray to hide the fact that I was gay. I also hid how certain creative activities excited me and never fully expressed how I wanted to sing more, dance more, and play with dolls more, and just whatever activity I thought was fun as a child to really explore was stunted because I was afraid of being me.

CHAPTER 4. NASHVILLE

My mother was a P.E. Teacher, and they went on a field trip to Nashville and she absolutely loved it! She saw how different things were, she saw the potential, but even more, she wanted better for me and my sister, and my daddy. When she got back, she immediately told us we are moving to Nashville. I seriously thought she was kidding, but she was dead serious. It was less than a month later, we were packing up our stuff and getting ready for the move. I was okay with it as long as we were coming back, but my mom just said we'd come back, but little did I know she just meant to visit. I was just getting use to my hiding, and I was looking forward to growing better as a basketball player to continue to humiliate my bullies and grow up with the few good friends I had.

Nashville was different, but still the same in the type of treatment I received. The other kids would always recognize that I was different and always say, "Oh, he a sissy," but little did they know I was ready for it... I didn't care what they had to say, and I'd always give them chances to leave me alone. My sister was developing as a young lady, extremely popular with a lot of friends, smart, pretty, and athletic, so she wasn't around as much to be my shield so I start beating people's asses. I was fighting multiple times a year, and my mama would always take my music away, which at the time I was infatuated with Bone Thugs N Harmony. I didn't have a lot of close friends like she did, so I would often tag along on her playdates because her friends would often have brothers. They didn't want to hang with me, they'd hear me talk and immediately give me this weird look. It was basketball that made them show me some respect. They played a different style game here, and it intrigued me. My game was more fundamental and solid, and theirs was a bit street and flashy—a combination of very fast dribbling and crafty moves that I quickly absorbed and used against them. I think it's funny that it's still a group of those guys who I actually see from time to time who like to credit any little hype that started to generate around my name and basketball to them teaching me, if it helps them sleep better at night, I don't care. But I also never forgot how they never invited me to anything, never wanted to hang out with me besides competing on the basketball court, and the fact that they would call me a sissy and punk.

I only had a couple of friends—a Black kid named Mark who reminded me of Deon from Arkansas. Me and Mark really just hung out at school; he would make fun of me sometimes, but he was always lighthearted about it. It was like a big brother picking on his little brother, and we'd always just laugh and have fun. Mark also knew I wasn't a punk, so anytime someone would come around trying to pick on me, he'd be the first to let them know they better leave me alone. We enjoyed playing with and against each other on the basketball court at school, and we just had a solid friendship. My other friend was this crazy ass White kid named Bonny. There were bad kids in Arkansas, but the kids in Nashville were really bad. They were smoking weed, drinking, stealing, and just doing bad shit, and Bonny fell into that category. Bonny knew I was different, but he didn't care; he actually talked funny almost to the point that you thought he was a child with special needs, but he was fully aware of it and he got made fun of for it, and I can't help but feel that's why he was so cool with me. We got picked on, but Bonny was crazy; not only would he fight you but he was getting expelled from school for trying to stab people who would mess with him. We never had any problems; it was just a mutual respect. I'd always enjoy hearing his stories about the crazy shit he'd be doing, and he just loved being on my team when we would play basketball at the makeshift basketball court at the apartments. Transitioning into middle school, I ended up losing touch with both of them, as Mark was in a further part of town and Bonny ended up moving out of state.

Middle school was just as crazy as you'd think it would be; a bunch of bad ass kids that you can't tell nothing! I was back to hiding under basketball, rapping, and stealing shit. I had got good with stealing, and this is when malls were around. The neighborhood we were growing up in had a few drug dealers, and I always thought they looked so cool and they had all the pretty, popular girls. I would go to the mall and steal FUBU,

15

Phat Farm, Karl Kani, and Tommy Hilfiger. It helped take the edge off people assuming I was gay. The girls still could smell it out, but the bullying started to ease off because between my sister being so popular and certain popular kids hanging with me and people knowing I could ball, they just thought I was cool, so much so I actually won homecoming king! During the summer, I played on an older AAU team, and a lot of the players on my team grew up in the projects. They didn't take it easy on me, they never missed a chance to call me a sissy, and they were always joking on each other. I'd always try to avoid them because they were ruthless, funny but ruthless. All of them were extremely talented too, not just in basketball but really anything they wanted to put their mind to, and I recognized that, unfortunately, a large majority got caught up in the trap—some are dead, some are in jail, and some are doing just fine. My life was being led by all these influences of what I thought I needed to be. I picked up so many bad habits to hide who I was. I smoked weed when I was twelve, I was acting like somebody I wasn't, I was being bullied and humiliated by players who were bigger, stronger, and just overall better than me, and a lot of my actions were being shaped by these environments. I was such a young fraud, liar, and thief, and even though I was able to handle my own by acting out, I can't help but feel like some type of self-hate and resentment was building up.

CHAPTER 5. FAMILY ISSUES

My dad hated being in Nashville. It was clear he did not like the big city, and my mom was taking advantage of all the opportunities that made her relocate us. They were always arguing, but it was only because my mother wanted better, she wanted better for him, she wanted better for us... She did what she could to get him out the house and introduce him to people and network, but he would always have a borderline panic attack. There was this one time we went to this church, and this White man was having a very open sincere conversation with him, and my dad had on this light purple shirt that was damn near soaked with sweat because he was so nervous. I didn't know how to feel because I'd think of those times he would antagonize me, but I also thought about the times when he was just a good dad picking us up from school, bringing food home and cooking, making us laugh and just being himself, and seeing him panic like that would always make me think, *what's the matter with my daddy?* My father continued working the only job I've known him to have which was a cook at Hardee's, and my mom busted her ass even more and picked up a second job to get us out those apartments and into a house. During this time, me and my sister were making that transition into high school, and it was a critical point in both of our lives. That summer, I went to a basketball camp at a private school named Ezell Harding. I dominated that camp. The coach made it a point to always speak to my mom every day; he wanted me there, he questioned why I had been playing out of position, and that he would prefer me to work with their point guards and play varsity. It excited me because on all the other teams I was playing on, they just wanted me to play on the block, told me I couldn't shoot, and just rebound. But here it was the exact opposite—the varsity players wanted to play with me; the other guards both Black and White wanted to make me better and told me how practice would be and that they thought I'd have a good chance of maybe starting as a freshman. It was a level of support and confidence I'd never experienced. When they broke down the scholarship package, my parents still needed to pay about $400 a month to send me there, and my mom really wanted me to go, but she could not afford it... I knew the competition was better at my public high school and I wanted that challenge, but this was also an opportunity for me to be around a group of people who had not once bullied me, called me a sissy, and really respected the potential of my game. This is important to understand because as I got older, I grew to resent my father more and more, especially as my high school basketball career played out with each year becoming more toxic than the next. He was supposed to be able to pro-vide that experience for me to be able to attend that private school where I was wanted and had that rare experience of not having player haters. He needed to be there and recognize the type of team I needed to play for; there was a level of support and confidence I needed from my father, and IT WAS NOT THERE! It also didn't help that he had just fully given up and succumbed to drugs. He went from sleeping in the bed with mother, to sleeping on their bedroom floor, to sleeping on the couch, to sleeping in his car! When me and my sister would talk to him about it, he'd bluff it off and just say some shit like "your mama need her space" or "she don't want me in the house." He eventually stopped showing up, and my mom went looking for him and found him with some crack head, and she lost it! She came home and grabbed the biggest kitchen knife we had and left. My sister called my granny and I swear her, and my Auntie were in Nashville in less than two hours and Nashville is at least a four-hour drive from Forrest City! When they got there, they went driving around the city trying to find her and ended up finding out that my dad had been spotted in Memphis and my mom was too! She had apparently been chasing them and was going to kill them, but my granny was able to talk her down. I just remember my mom getting back home around 4 a.m. the next morning, and when she walked through the door, it looked like she had literally walked through hell... Her eyes were blood-shot red; her hair was a mess; she looked sweaty and grimy and just flat out over this world. I remember my granny calling her name "Charlotte..." and she went to her room and slammed her door. It would be four years before we saw our father again...

19

High School flew by... And I all I could think about was just not letting people find out I was gay. I was developing as a young man and I had a lot of girls who genuinely liked me, but I shifted my focus to just doing my schoolwork, working my little summer jobs, and playing basketball. I always used that as an excuse anytime people would ask me about girls. Things really weren't that bad. The development of the Internet played on my curiosity of the gay world, and looking back, this was the early stages of what all these hookup apps are today like Grindr, etc. But during that time, it was more so these themed AOL chat rooms, and you know my curiosity led me to searching gay chats... Once again, I was on there doing stuff I had no business doing; my early exposure to porn as a child led me to searching gay porn and I found some stuff. There was this one time I didn't clear the history, and it led to a video my sister found; it was blurry and both men had long blonde hair, so the sex scene looked like a straight couple. My sister yelled for me to come into the room and asked what is this mess on the computer! I lied and told her I didn't know; she knew I was lying. I was just scared to death that she was so close to finding out. Even though me and my sister were super close, she never questioned me about my sexuality, but there was this one time in church where I was just messing with her, and she was already mad because she and mama had one of their moments of arguing that morning for whatever reason, and I'm not sure what I did, but it obviously pissed her off because I just remember her turning to me and saying, "Shut your gay ass up." I was hurt. I asked her "what did you say?" And she just ignored me. Between my feelings being hurt, I also thought, damn, she just cussed in church and called me gay. Anyway, those damn chat rooms were the go-to for all the closet gays in the city. I had two meet-ups as a sixteen-year-old boy and what was I doing? What was I thinking? Nothing happened, they just took me out to eat and talked with me; they knew I wasn't of age. I'm actually still friends with one of them and he called me out on my bullshit; I'd lie in the chat and say I was eighteen, but when we met up, he asked for my ID and I was caught, but he was cool about it. I ended up eventually chatting with one guy who went to high school with me; we met up and I kissed a guy for the first time; he was a tad bit on the fem side and that didn't really turn me on, but he was a sweetheart. He also kissed and told because he knew I played basketball; he spilled the beans to me about a former superstar basketball player from our school. I couldn't believe it! In a way, I was kind of jealous because not only was he a star, I was told he also had a huge penis! So here I am thinking, he can hoop, swinging pipe, and I'm sure he's getting all the boys at the major D1 school he was playing ball. I was slick hating. I also was kind of saddened—he and I didn't have a chance to connect more about being Black and gay, and we both hooped! But ironically, that chance would present itself later on in the future.

Hate was more so in the workplace. I realized it, but honestly, it didn't faze me especially considering all the name calling and bullying I experienced in my early childhood. And I knew my destiny was so much more; these people, these haters were lowlifes and I knew they were scum; I couldn't keep a job, I'd always let their disrespect build up, and I'd snap.

I'd always end up calling my momma to come pick me, and she'd just shake her head and be like, "Boo what happened this time..."

CHAPTER 6. COLLEGE

My last year of high school was not bad but it was the worse out of the four years there. My high school coach loved me and my hustle, and he was always using me as a prototype example. However, the other players didn't respect me; after all I was an undersized power forward, and I was never really an all-star. People knew I could ball, but my true potential never really showed in games; younger players were averaging more points than me, and the other guards did all the scoring. Looking at my averages of just six points six rebounds a game, you'd think I just sucked. I got invited to go play in front of some small NAIA schools after the season, and I did pretty good, so much so that one offered me a split athletic/academic scholarship. I was excited about going to college! I just remember watching all the different movies and TV shows about how college life is, and I was looking forward to it... I mainly just cared about basketball because I was determined to work my way into the player rotation; my first year was supposed to be as a red shirt to develop as a guard, but when I got to campus that fall and at all the open runs, I dominated all the other red shirts. So much so that the veteran players would come watch me play and go back and talk to coach and say he needs to be playing now. When I say those were some of the happiest moments of my life, those were some of the happiest moments of my life! I would always call home to my mama and tell her how the other players were excited about watching me play and that coach was talking to me about not being a red shirt that year. I worked hard. Coach came to me and said that I'd be traveling with the team and would dress out, but he didn't want me to waste my redshirt year, but it was a possibility that I might be playing that year. Ecstatic! I was the top freshman! The veteran players all showed me love. They all were like big brothers, and I looked up to all them. I respected all their games, a lot of them were D1 rejects, All Star JuCo players, and a couple of crowned bench rider redshirts from the previous years. They respected my potential and all of them were just cool. They knew I was different, but they didn't say anything at first. They just saw I was hungry to play and they respected that… When the season first started, we won our first game, and in the locker room, they were so hype and rowdy and yelled, "Tonight 301!" "301!" I'm like what is 301? 301 was one of the dorm rooms that a few of my teammates were all sharing and that was the party room! I remember getting to that party and it was alcohol, weed, girls, music, card games, and just that classic college party like I'd seen on TV. The whole time I kept thinking about the practice the next day. They didn't care. I had a few drinks and was just watching, taking in the moment. It was a fun time. The next day at practice, coach already knew what was up; he was pissed, and he could literally smell the alcohol coming out of our pores as he ran us for two hours! As the season went on, it was clear I was the only player on the team not fucking no girls. They knew. Between all the crazy locker room talk and the super small campus, everybody knew everybody's business. They would blurt out from time to time that Randolph is gay, but it wasn't like before when I was growing up being bullied. They said it in a way like it's okay, man, you can tell us! But I'd always lie and say I'm not gay and laugh it off. When we would go on road trips, the star players would always come talk to me and say that I needed to go to a JuCo and just build my confidence up as a guard and that they felt that I really had a chance to play mid D-1; those were some proud moments, and from time to time, they'd straight up ask me, "Randolph, are you gay?" I'd just look at them like they were crazy. I think it was a challenge between all of them to see who was going to get me to come out, but I was determined to stay in the closet, I wasn't at that point ready to really express myself but it was coming... One of my teammates, this crazy White boy who I thought was attractive, at the half time of our games would always "spssst!" whisper at me and pull back his shorts and show me his dick and balls. I was shocked and liked it all at the same time. Shocked because nobody else saw him doing this, coach would be up there writing and yelling at the board, half the team paying attention and the other half just looking off into space, and here he is pulling back his shorts showing me his dick. What a tease! He did it one time in practice when we had a rest break after running suicides and I got hard! I had to run to the back because the erection was showing. When I came back out on the court, his

25

face was cherry red from laughing so hard. He knew. And I feel like this was some ole red neck country White boy shit that they did to tease the queers because this would not be the only time I experienced this; one of the baseball boys would stop by my room and do it too… it's like a straight boy seeing a nice pair of titties, just being flashed at him. Crazy thing is nobody ever saw him do it! But I do think he told his girlfriend because I would always see them together on campus and they would always giggle walking past me. And I knew how crazy he was and his girlfriend played on the soccer team which was a team full of lesbians, so I'm sure she experimented at some point, and she had this borderline crazed look in her eyes too, so I knew she was just as crazy, if not crazier than him.

When I wasn't playing basketball, I was kicking it with the other redshirts and always staring at the baseball boys. I thought they were so hot. They would always come into the cafeteria with those tight baseball pants on or some loose shorts and I was just thirsty. Wondering if one of them might be like me. All the freshmen had a separate dorm from the rest of the campus, and all the other redshirt basketball players stayed on the third floor, and the majority of the baseball players were on the second floor where I was staying. After long days at practice and being in the library, I'd walk the hallways and make random conversations with them; everybody would always keep their doors wide open, playing music, video games, cooking on their George Foremans, just a freshman frat house. I ended up stopping at one of the baseball guys' rooms who had a Super Nintendo, and we instantly connected on that. I've always given myself the title of the best Super Nintendo player in the world, and he had a few of my favorite games that he swore he could beat me in and I'd always whoop his ass. His name was Gavin. I sincerely liked Gavin as my friend; we would just have good convo talking about our high school days and our families, listening to some Bone Thugs and 3-6 Mafia, and of course playing Super Nintendo. He thought I was the coolest muthafucker ever—that's how he introduced me to his best friend, and he was always happy to let people know I was in his room. My little reputation of being the redshirt freshman that's not really a redshirt freshman on the basketball team was a highlight of the campus. Eventually, other baseball players started to come to Gavin's room when they knew I was in there because they wanted to be around the coolest muthafucker ever, and that's when I spotted one of them just staring at me. We caught eyes, and he was just giving me this stank look like what's the hype about this guy. I made sure not to stare too long because when I first saw him, I immediately thought, JESUS CHRIST HE IS SO FUCKING HOT! His name was Luke. What made it even more fascinating was that every time I would go to hang out in Gavin's room, Luke would come too because his room was directly across from his, and everyone always kept their doors open, so he knew when I was there. It got to a point that when Luke would come in, he'd always say little smart comments and I'd ignore him on purpose. I wanted Luke to keep messing with me and he did; the more I acted like I didn't care for what he was saying, the more he would say. I found it even more fascinating when Luke wasn't around, Gavin would tell me Luke only comes to his room when I'm there; so I knew he was there just to see me. Going into that second semester, me and Luke had Biology together. Our classes were small, and there were plenty of desks to choose from. I was in class early, and when Luke came in, he sat directly beside me. I remember just looking at him and he looked back and said "What???" I don't think he knew what he was in for... He thought I was going to be that passive guy who was just going to act like he didn't care for what he was saying, but I knew I was going to flirt my ass off. And flirt I did. He wasn't ready. At that time, the Mariah Carey song "We Belong Together" was a hit, and I asked him if he liked that song and had he seen the video, and he said he liked it too and that Mariah Carey was hot... I said, "fuck Mariah, did you see that guy in the video now he was hot!" Luke lost it! He said, "What did you say?!?!" I was like, "the guy, the guy she went running to, he is hot as hell!" He looked at me like I was crazy. I was just getting started. I would bring up different movies that had guys I was attracted to, and just go on and on talking about these men and how attractive they were. I started saying all kinds of crazy sexual stuff anytime our professor would ask the class a question, but no one ever heard it except Luke. This was hilarious. Because I was literally saying ridiculous stuff out loud, and no one seemed to hear it except Luke. For example, the professor would say something like what does molecule D stand for, and I'd say "Dick," and look right at Luke; his eyes would get so big and he'd start looking around the room and back at me, and I'd just be looking right back at him with a raised eyebrow. There was one time I said something ridiculous, and he turned to one of the girls and said, "did you hear him?" She said, "hear what?" It was so funny. I remember he would go back to the dorms and tell all the other baseball guys how I was basically harassing him with constantly talking about men and gay sex, but when they would ask me about it, I would act clueless. This drove him crazy. He knew I was fucking with him big time. I eventually stopped going to Gavin's room and instead went to Luke's room and just started hanging out. We hit it off as friends. Luke ass was crazy too; we'd talk about other people on campus; I'd only disclose to him his teammates I thought were attractive, and it just got to a point where we just had that little bond. Because if he tried to call me out on my shit in front of people, I'd always play dumb and he'd just look silly. At that time, Luke was a good boy. He didn't go out to any parties and really just did his work, played baseball, hung out at the dorms, rinse and repeat. Going into our sophomore year, that changed. Luke started drinking and going to parties. I was always excited to see him out, and he'd get excited to see me. We'd just have a good time laughing and just being at the party with everybody, but nothing would never happen. Luke ended up transferring to ETSU, a bigger school, because he felt like The College was too small and that he was missing out on a real college experience. He had a group of friends there that he ended up partying hard with, and he'd always invite me out to come party there, but I never really had a chance to because of basketball. We kept in close touch; we'd always text each other, and he'd text stuff like I miss you man and I love you. It always made me smile. I eventually had a chance to make it to one of those parties at his new school, and we ended up staying to the end of one of the parties that a couple of girls had threw. The majority of people were starting to leave, and me and Luke were just hanging out in the living room on the couch, and there was this girl in the kitchen who had stepped away to go to the bathroom. When Luke realized it was just us there, he grabbed me and kissed me. What a moment! He heard the bathroom door open and immediately pushed off of me. I was just looking in shock. He punched me and gave me this look like "act like nothing happened." I ended up leaving shortly after and was just confused and happy. We never talked about that moment; it just happened, and for the most part our friendship, we just carried on as usual, but going into that summer, he told me that he was coming back to The College. That made me happy knowing that he was going to be around again. Luke had got to a point where he was a little party animal. I wanted to test him and I invited him to go to the gay club with me. He was a bit reluctant at first, but I told him it would be a lot of fun and he could just stay near me and that he'd be fine. I also warned him that he'd get a lot of attention and that a lot of the guys would probably stare at him and probably offer to buy him drinks. He said if anybody did offer free drinks, he'd take it… When we stepped into that club, it was like Tom Cruise walked in there. When I say all eyes were on Luke, all eyes were on Luke. I remember him whispering everybody is staring at us, and I was thinking, no, everybody is staring at you! I knew this because I had been to the gay club only a few times with one of the guys I met back offline when I was sixteen. He waited until I was eighteen and took me out to the gay club, and I got stared at but not like how they looked at Luke. That's how I knew all eyes were on him. We were in there less than five minutes, and multiple guys were inching their way toward us, every single one of them offering to buy us drinks. I know you're thinking we weren't old enough to drink, but we had fake IDs that had us over twenty-one. Terrible, I know. But, we were the talk of the club. Luke stayed by my side the entire time, and any time someone would try to talk to him, he'd always grab me and be like this is my friend Randolph. I could immediately look at those men in their eyes and just see the lust they had for Luke. I wasn't jealous at that time because Luke was with me. We danced a bit and were able to get drinks from whoever we wanted; we caught the drag shows and ended up leaving. It was a fun night! But that attention was like crack to Luke. I found out later he was going out there on his own; he had met a group of guys and eventually started hanging out with them quite a bit. The summer of our Junior year, Luke was heavy on to the scene; neither one of us was out and Luke bounced between hanging with his straight friends from college and the gay boys from the club. I didn't say anything and would go out with him from time to time. There was one night we went out, and there was one bartender both me and Luke liked. His name was Aidan; that night, Aidan got off work early and tagged along with me and Luke. Aidan eventually pulled me aside, and I ended up going home with him. During this time, anytime men would make a move on me, I wasn't having sex with them because I was deathly afraid of HIV. And a lot of times, when hookups would happen, most guys would try to pull my bare dick into them and I'd always just say no, so it was just a lot of foreplay going at this time. Aidan was the only guy I thought was just as hot as Luke, and I had him, us two laying naked together; I was borderline mesmerized. So much so that this led to me coming out. I didn't want to hide it anymore. Aidan was such a free spirit and I appreciated it; it gave me the courage to do it. I told my sister first, then my mother, and all my close friends. If anybody asked me if I were gay, I'd tell them. I wasn't afraid anymore.

I was looking forward to going into my Junior year of college. When I wasn't working that summer, I was working on my game, and I was playing some of the best basketball of my life. I was feeling confident as a point guard and just being myself considering I had come out. I had found out that we were getting a new coach, and he wanted to meet up with me and he told me he had heard a lot of good things about me and that I had nothing to worry about as far as it concerned my spot on the team. That man lied to me in my face. It was just a week later he said that there would be a tryout; about twelve guys were there from his old school and I gave all of them work! It was clear I was one of the best players on the floor. This man put a final roster list up, and I was not on there. I was devastated. My sports management professor was upset and even suggested I transfer. I had other players coming to apologize to me, and the whole campus just realizing I was just done dirty. I decided to stay. The game of basketball is something that I love to play. I love playing basketball. I knew I was better than half the players on that team, and that's all that mattered to me. I played intramurals and just had fun with that. I had my best game against that new coach who also was playing intramurals, and I just remember him looking at me like he made a mistake. His assistant coach had a private talk with me and told me the head coach told him that cutting me was one of his biggest regrets in his coaching career; those words meant nothing to me and still don't. I have no respect for that man as a coach and never will until he apologizes to me in my face just like how he lied to me in my face.

My school was in Pulaski, TN, home of the KKK, and I just remember people coming up with questions such as, "How can you go to school down there?" "Are they racist?" "How does everyone treat you?" Funny thing is being on campus was actually fun for me. I made the best of it; it wasn't until I had got cut from the basketball team that the insidious traits of that campus started to show itself. I lost the scholarship money from playing basketball when I got cut, but they partially subsidized it with an academic one. Another one of my good friends on campus at the time who was Black came to me and was extremely disappointed and sad because he had also lost his basketball money, and the college financial aid advisor told him that there was nothing they could do about it. My friend was upset because he was going to have to take out more loans, and the only thing he could think of was how in the hell was he ever going to repay it. It was only a week later, I had a discussion with Gavin who came to me and was bouncing off the wall excited because he was going to have to take a break from school because he didn't have the money to cover his tuition and was told by the college financial aid advisor, "how about we make up a scholarship for you?" They literally just gave him the money! I've always kept this to myself until now because I didn't know how to process it. I knew it was fucked up. I knew it wasn't right. I knew it didn't make sense. There was more corruption. I always prided myself on my writing in English class, and there was this one professor who only gave me D's and F's on my papers, and I didn't understand it. I went and spoke with him, and he would give me these bullshit excuses that didn't make sense to me. I'd ask to look at my other White classmates' papers who were making A's, and after reading their work, I realized my work was just as good, if not better than theirs; it got to a point that I was meticulously scanning my papers to ensure nothing was wrong, and this man never gave me anything higher than a C. My final grade for that class was a D. The next semester, one of the White baseball boys knew I had that professor and had a repeat assignment that I had written a paper for, and he asked me if I had it and he was just going to copy it and turn it in. I told him I did but that I had a D on it and that he wouldn't want it. He didn't care; he just wanted something to turn in, so I gave it to him. A week later, he came to me apologizing and showed me the paper, and he received an A– and a paragraph about how great the paper was… I just had that blank stare feeling again. To me, this was a silent, invisible hate. Not only did I know these moments were wrong but deep down my blood was slowly boiling. A body full of mixed emotions realizing that I am dealing with an enemy. To make matters worse, there was one night I went to one of the baseball boys' houses who was throwing a huge party. Everybody was there. A couple of my good friends had gotten really drunk and just needed to go home. I drove them both home, and on my way back, I drove through a stop sign to park; the baseball boy's house was literally right after the stop sign. I parked, and as I was getting out of the car, police lights started flashing, and they got out and told me I just ran the stop sign. I let them know that I was parking and that I was at my destination and I was spending the night there. They completely ignored me, took me through the routine, and proceeded to give me a field sobriety test, in which they said I failed. One of the White baseball boys came running out the house, letting the police have it, cussing them out, telling them they were wrong, and just flat out giving them hell! They arrested him too but then let him go. I was told that I should go see one of the campus advisors—let's just call him Dr. Pedo… I swear Dr. Pedo had a bigger crush on all the baseball boys than I did. He did all sorts of inappropriate things but only with the White baseball and soccer boys— Bought them liquor, took them on trips, gave them money, asked inappropriate questions about girls to see if they even liked girls, and was just flat out grooming them to possibly one day get his disgusting faggot dreams filled of hooking up with one of the hot White college boys. He disgusted me, and I knew he was gay. Every inappropriate thing he did, they told me, but they also told me how well connected this man was and that I was not going to have worry about the DUI. I went to the lawyer he suggested, and he charged me $2,500 and I ended up being charged with a first offense DUI, had to pay a fine, and do forty-eight hours in jail. That was the standard conviction. I later found out from another lawyer who was recommended to me from my good friend I met off the Internet when I was sixteen, that I got screwed over and that he basically just took my money. She told me that I should not have gone to jail, that he could have gotten that charge reduced to reckless driving, paid a small fine and that's it. She was more furious than I was. I once again had that blank stare feeling again. Realizing I was dealing with this hidden hate.

I was starting to see Pulaski, TN for what it was historically known for... I always think of that scene from the *Malcom X* movie when Malcolm has flashbacks of certain White men in his life who are in these leadership positions and constantly telling him that he's not worthy. That was the feeling I had in my last few semesters of college. However, I was determined to graduate and just be done with that deceitful place, but not everyone was bad. I had some great professors who genuinely loved and helped me and I made some lifelong friends.

My college crush Luke was going through it too; social media was just starting to pop off, mainly Facebook, and some fake profile took it upon themselves to out Luke. Saying that he has been going to gay bars, that he doesn't like girls, and that he was just flat out gay! They sent it to everybody. Luke came to me crying and seriously wanted to kill himself. Considering that I had recently come out, I just told him that it's not that bad and that nobody cares! Seriously, nobody cared. I had a few people come to me telling me that they had received the social media blasts outing Luke, but they were just okay about it. He's gay. And... Not only that but all his baseball buddies rallied around him and nothing changed. I was happy for him. That spring break, the whole campus was going down to Panama City. I went with my basketball friends and Luke went with his baseball boys. The whole time I was just thinking I wanted to party with Luke. Spring Break was Spring Break! There were parties everywhere! Fun, fun, and more fun! I was doing my thing with my group and Luke was with his, but we were messaging each other and found out that we were going to be at the same party that night. I just remember walking in and the place being packed, music blasting, and college kids partying like how college kids party! Walking through the crowds, I spotted Luke; he eventually swung around and saw me and started waving for me to come his way. I made my way through, and we got to talking, and then one of my favorite artists at the time came on, The-Dream/Falsetto. Luke knew I loved that song and knew I loved dancing to it; we just looked at each other and I just led the way. We danced to it; I made sure not to leave him hanging on the rhythm by grabbing his hands and showing him my choreography, and we took the spotlight; it's funny because this wouldn't be the last time we'd do this. But after we shut that song down, we both just wanted to get out of there and we did. We were trying to figure out whose hotel was closer and his was, but once we got there, we both realized we were sharing the room with our friends, and we ended up going in his hotel hallway and we were just going at it kissing each other; this girl turned the corner and you would have thought she saw a ghost by how shocked see looked to see these buff Black and White guys making out. We just gathered ourselves and ended up going to Luke's truck and continued there. Nothing other than us getting naked and continuing to make out happened, and we ended up passing out. We woke up the next morning; his truck was parked on the side of some random road, and we were both just kind of bewildered by what happened the previous night. It wasn't awkward, but it was just a moment that we both realized that we were better as friends. We talked about what had happened, but I can't help but feel like everything that led up to that moment was more of a brotherhood. We were like brothers. I feel as if the intimate moments we had just gave us confirmations of "Yes, I love you, but not like that." We decided at that moment that we were going to be best friends and little did we know that was going to set us up for even more epic adventures.

My last couple of semesters of college were very limited as I was doing an internship in Nashville and working too… I only cared about graduating and moving on to that next phase of life and that's what I did. I think it's funny how I was dealing with the bag of emotions that I was, and I put it in my final college speech and figured it would be a great way to end this chapter…

LOOK INTO MY EYES

You can't judge a book by its cover until you look into a person's eyes and tell them what you see. There is this one guy who I judge all the time because I constantly look him in his eyes, especially on certain occasions. These staring moments made me see life for what it really is… We spend our days among a variety of people, diverse cultures, complex and many ideas, and we are all left in a surrounding judging each other based on the past and present, stereotypes, and careless influence. The journeys I take from looking into this person's eyes has me judging forever.

I looked into his red-stained eyes and saw that he was upset with himself because he was not above the influence. He fell victim to the peer pressures of life and was deeply engulfed by the potent smoke. Looking into his fire eyes, I could see paranoia, the frustrations, the stress, the relief… Overwhelmed by such feeling, his eyes, his actions, swears he sees the highways of the world, and then I judge him. These feelings were powerful, and his brain was an open discussion, but he wanted to understand more on this distorted reality. The only way for that to happen was to take these levels to a new HIGH! I could see through his hypnosis that he was smarter than that and he would use this current state of euphoria to understand why not to pursue other forms of false realities in higher recreations.

I looked into his drowning eyes and saw a sad state of emotions and depression confused with joy. The dangers of this drunkenness are harmful and have more than proven to be fatal. Looking into his eyes, I just see waterfalls, but why? I start to judge him. I know that his father departed his life during a crucial part of his childhood that could have developed him to be a better man and to help him make proper decisions. He swears he is not affected by not having his father present his whole life, but he is. Intoxicated, I see that his sexual feelings are somewhat confused, not understanding why, but maybe it's something we all can't comprehend but need to get along with. I see he's devastated by having a passion unfairly revoked from him that he was willing to let go of at the right time. I see him upset with the world because he feels somebody owes him something when they really don't. However, I see through his blurred vision that moderation is key and he understands this. You can't stay drunk on the hardships of life but instead take control of your situation responsibly.

I look into his sober eyes and I see someone who will continue to learn from his mistakes. Realizing that, I judge him. His eyes, clear as day, reveal to me someone who is willing to think, grow, dream, and lead. Hard work is something that he has been faced with since the day of his birth, because society has placed judgments in the minds of people of what he ought to be like. Obstacles is what he calls it; the misjudgments and actions of others are something he does not understand and will not try to, but instead, he will focus on becoming a better person himself. He is full of self-confidence and will not be discouraged by failure. Life is a long journey for some, and he is eager to befriend people who are blind to flaws as we all have them. But who am I to judge him… But then again who am I not to.

Every time I looked him in his eyes, I was facing a mirror, staring at myself. You can't judge a book by its cover until you look into a person's eyes and tell them what you see and that person should be yourself. When people judge each other, it causes problems; therefore, we should be concerned with giving ourselves our own verdict and strive for improvement. Nobody has the right to judge anyone.

CHAPTER 7. IT'S COMPLICATED

When I graduated college, I was stuck between a rock and a hard place. I didn't know exactly what to do, and it didn't make it any better that the country had gone to hell with one of the worst recessions in history. I was employed at a sports retail store hoping to make my way up through the ranks to hopefully get the coolest job at The Big Sports Corporation at that time, which was a Brand Ambassador position. But this job basically was a marketing position that worked with everyone from the retail level on up to top events including the Olympics promoting all things Big Sports Corporation! I also was working part-time at a cellular corporation. During this time, I was contemplating going to graduate school as well but didn't have the money to pay for it and I really didn't want to jump through the hoops to be begging for scholarships, so I just kept working. I would go out from time to time, and one night, I spotted an attractive older gentleman. I just remember seeing him across the bar, and he was staring at me and kept whispering back to his friend looking at me. I figured I'd walk past and make conversation because it was clear he was interested, and I was too… I used to watch CNN because I always thought Anderson Cooper was sexy and he favored him. When I walked by, he gave me a little tap and said, "Hey!" He was an instant flirt. I liked it. And he was nice. We talked a bit and danced, and he told me he was staying in a hotel not too far from the bar and I left with him. It was a good time, nothing crazy, just a lot of foreplay and we got off. He told me how he traveled a lot for work and that he frequented middle Tennessee quite often, so we stayed in touch. His name was Gabe Powers. Gabe was a banker from Minnesota; he knew how to talk to anyone and was an extremely smart and sweet man. White men from the south just didn't interact with me the way he did… When he would have his trips to Tennessee, I'd make time to go see him. He also played on a traveling volleyball team, and I'd make trips to go to his tourneys when he was playing nearby as well. I liked Gabe. I liked the fact that he was older, wiser, more mature, but he was also at a different point in his life. I took a trip to Minnesota to go visit him, and he introduced me to a lot of his friends and family, showed me around the city, and really just treated me to a great time. He also challenged my thinking. I remember he showed me a picture of his previous boyfriend, and I couldn't get over how attractive he was. I Facebook stalked him and not only was he hot but it was also very clear the man was extremely successful. So I immediately was stuck on the thought of why does he want my broke Black ass? When Gabe showed me around the city, we stopped and looked at the house they were going to get together, and all I could do was gulp; it was a really nice house, and I knew I was nowhere near that level financially to even consider a house like that; looking back, I question myself why would I think like that if we really liked each other? Gabe would ask me questions on my beliefs of God and how I felt about religion. Did I really know what was going on in this world and how it works, where did I see myself in five years, etc.? As far as I was concerned, I just knew we lived in a fucked-up world. I couldn't quite articulate it back then, but as I've gotten older, my views have just been confirmed; we do indeed live in a fucked-up world. We ended up having another discussion closer to the end of my trip, and I told him how much I liked him, and he gave possibilities of helping me look at opportunities for me to move to Minnesota, and he also expressed his concern with how young I was and felt I needed to live more. I didn't like that he doubted my ability to grow into that relationship, and it hurt my feelings, but I also respected the fact that he didn't want to be my daddy either. We ended on good terms and still keep in touch on a random basis.

Shortly after breaking communication with Gabe Powers, I met Maxi Milian. It was in similar fashion as I met Gabe being out at the bars, but this time it was me who initiated everything. I just remember seeing Maxi standing out in the crowd. He was tall six feet three inches, and I could tell by looking at him that he was not from this country. I was intrigued and I made my way toward him. I tapped him on his shoulder, and when he turned and looked at me, he just stared. I knew he liked me. He spoke and his deep German accent confirmed all the preconceived thoughts I had about him. He was with some little short nerdy guy who kept jumping in the middle of our conversation. It was so annoying; I just remember Maxi constantly apologizing for his pesky friend. We ended up just swapping numbers that night and went from there. Maxi was so different. Our time together was all about conversation. I would always go visit him at his apartment and just hang out. He was a music student at Belmont, and we would talk about his classes, his on-campus job, and I'd always vent to him about how I hated working at the cellular store and my aspirations with The Big Sports Corporation. He was so inquisitive and could squeeze ten questions out of one. Maxi had a way of showing me that he cared about me as a human being and I liked that. It was like we were both always looking to find out how we could maximize the time in our days when we were not busy being together. Some of my favorite moments would be when we just lay together on the floor, his head on my chest, holding each other's hands—it was a good energy and I loved it. A whole month went by before we ever made a move on each other, and those were always special moments. Mainly just a lot of passionate kissing. All of this would be short lived. Maxi brought to my attention that he would be going back home to Germany, and I asked him when was he planning to return. He explained that his time at Belmont was done and that he'd be going back home for good. I was hurt. We had talked about him being from Germany, but clearly, I misunderstood that his time here was temporary. I was under the impression that he was here for good. We had our goodbyes, and I just wanted to forget about him to avoid facing my real feelings for him, and when he returned to Germany, I made it a point to ignore him. I figured I'd never see him again and didn't want to be reminded of how much I liked him.

Meanwhile after being with those two guys who I really liked and things not panning out as far as having a meaningful relationship, Luke was still in the picture as my right-hand man. He was critical of both Gabe and Maxi, but I didn't care what he had to say about either one of them because I liked them. Needless to say, he was glad when both of them were out of the picture because he had his running mate unbothered. Me and Luke were something else when we were together; people always thought we were dating but that was not the case. We just knew how to have a fun time! We were practically brothers, and I had no doubts about that as Luke had developed quite the reputation in the city and was able to get access to all the in crowds. Even with the ones who I thought were toxic because they treated me differently before they knew me and Luke were best friends. I even went as far as stealing Luke's old phones because I didn't trust some of the guys he was hanging with at the time and wanted to see how they talked about me. It was interesting how my name would always come up, and Luke would always go to bat for me in those texts, literally saying Randolph is like a brother to me and I love him, nothing more nothing less. Knowing that he let some of those guys, who I knew deep down didn't care for me and I'm sure hated me because of how close our friendship was, know who I was to him gave me real trust in Luke. Me and Luke would literally travel the country and party. Chicago, Orlando, Atlanta, but it was probably our trip to LA that was the most memorable.

There was one guy named Trevor who had an obsessive infatuation with me, but I didn't want anything more but to just be Trevor's friend. Trevor literally forced his way into Luke's and my friendship when he lived in Nashville, and Luke absolutely despised him, but I always played the peacemaker and just made sure everyone had a good time. Trevor had moved out to LA and invited us out to come party for Halloween. He told us that it's literally one of the biggest parties in the country. I told Luke about it and he agreed to go with me. I always thought it was hilarious how annoyed Luke was by Trevor, but he kept it together while we were in LA; there would be times we would have our little inside jokes about Trevor and would burst out laughing; it was nothing too cruel, no worse than us knowing that he always had ulterior motives for me that were always made blatant because Trevor would always get so pissed when he'd introduce us to some of his very attractive friends and there happened to be one who was semi-famous and a big flirt with me and I flirted back but more on that later… During our time there in LA, we were all over the city, eating at the trendy restaurants, playing ball at the parks, walking the strips, and going to the Big Sport stores, house parties, and last but not least, the clubs. Everyone knew about "The Abbey," and Luke and I didn't fall short to turn heads there. Trevor was obviously jealous but at the same time felt entitled simply because he knew he was with some studs. Trevor's semi-famous friend ended up catching up with us and took us around to a few other clubs, and we ended up at one that was playing all the good music. The type of music that I liked to dance to, and then they played this super sexy remix version of "Meet me Halfway" by the Black Eyed Peas. I quickly finished my drink and grabbed Luke and pulled him to the dance floor. He knew how much I liked that song and had seen me dance to it a million times, so much so that I didn't have to guide his dancing; he just caught on; that entire club formed a circle around us and we didn't miss a beat. Imagine being in Hollywood, partying in Hollywood, and creating a scene. That moment was so good, it was so hot, it was so memorable. When that song ended, if a man could get wet, I swear every pant in the club would have been soaking wet. All eyes were on us; people came asking who we were—if we were strippers, are we boyfriends, was this staged, offering us drinks, telling us where the next after party was and we should come. Meanwhile, Trevor was around like a little trolling bodyguard letting everyone know, "HEY, THEY ARE WITH ME!" It only helped my cause with Trevor's semi-famous friend as I ended up leaving and hooking up with him that night. That next day when I caught back up with Luke and Trevor, that dance scene was the only thing we could talk about; it was a special moment. Partying in Hollywood.

CHAPTER 8. MOVING ON

Luke's and my party phase started to ease up a bit; we both were making moves to further our careers. Luke had met a guy from Chicago who he was really head over heels for, and I knew it because we had multiple conversations about this guy, and I could tell how his voice tones would change when he spoke to me about him that he really liked this guy, so much so that he moved to Chicago to be with him. I was happy for Luke; he needed to settle down. I on the other hand had just gotten a job promotion that had me relocating to Louisville, KY. I had done a tremendous amount of networking and ended up getting a chance to interview for the Brand Ambassador position but didn't get it, but instead landed a specialist position in a brand-new store, which was basically just lower-level management. I was so excited! I felt like I was making small steps to achieve my goal of one day landing that Brand Ambassador job. My early days in that position were great. I enjoyed everything I was doing from shipping and receiving, training, learning about new products, taking on special initiatives, and truly living one of The Big Sports Corporation key tag lines of "Make Big Sports Corporation Exciting!" It was an awesome experience. My favorite thing to do was cheer, and I'd always hear certain songs and would remix them to fit in different things that were unique to the Big Sports Corporation culture and those moments were always so hype! I loved it. All that would come to an end, but I'll touch on that a little later. Basketball continued to be a gateway to learning the new city and meeting more people. Between playing against some co-workers and establishing a reputation at the local gyms, people were eager to get to know me. They knew I wasn't from the area and would invite me to private runs where I had a chance to play with some former UL players who played in the NBA, overseas, and a few who played on the 2013 National Championship team. I always admired these moments because it gave me confidence that I could play with anyone. I might not have ever been a superstar player, but the fact that I had consistently throughout my lifetime played with and gained respect from some of the best was all I needed. It was also good basketball. No fighting, no arguing, no ego—just a good fun run. I was really enjoying the experience of moving to Louisville.

The gay scene gave me a warm welcome as well. Keep in mind that a majority of the of the awesome experiences I had had on the gay scene in Nashville was largely because I was friends with Luke and everyone was willing to give Luke anything he wanted to gain an inch of his attention. The gay crowd in Louisville was a down-to-earth culture that embraced me with a lot of good energy. I ended up coming across a group of guys who reminded me of Luke and my friendship, as they had a lot of similar moments that we had. I would enjoy hearing their stories and how they became best friends and realized that friendship was best, how they met their partners, and just their overall welcoming spirit. I liked to call them the doctors as the majority of them were doctors. They were a popular group, and it was a couple of them who made moves on me and I hooked up with. I'm not sure if their partners knew, but I never intruded on their relationships, caught feelings, nothing was weird, nothing was messy. They would still invite me to their House/Derby parties, UL basketball games, and nights out, and everybody was just so cool.

A couple of years after being in Louisville, I received a message from Maxi Milian; something to keep in mind is that he had been sending me messages and trying to get in contact with me ever since he left, but I never responded; I ignored him. I didn't want to face those feelings. After compressing and neglecting those feelings I had when my father got turned out on drugs, having a cold heart became very easy for me, so when it came to strong feelings that I didn't want to deal with, I had a way of simply ignoring it, and that's what I was doing to Maxi. However, that day when he sent that random message just saying, "Randolph," I responded back with "Hello, Maxi." He was shocked, hurt, and pissed all at the same time. He sent multiple long messages telling me how much I hurt him and that he felt that our connection was so strong for me to treat him like he never existed, and it was. I went on to explain why I did what I did. He understood but also wanted us to try and work something out. I even suggested coming to Louisville to visit me and he did. It was good seeing him again. I felt those strong feelings coming back as we spent time together; it felt like when we first met. His level of understanding, concern, and overall intelligence always had a way of really making me happy; however, there was still some level of concern about how this relationship was going to carry on. We discussed our future and what it could look like; we talked about both monogamous and an open relationship. Maxi expressed how he was not quite ready to commit to a monogamous relationship, which honestly took me for a surprise. I didn't quite understand how that could be an issue considering the feelings we shared for each other. I knew the distance would factor in, but I wanted us to take that next step whether that be him coming to America or me going to Germany, and he could never give me a concrete answer but more so a lot of doubt. I did not like that and I felt my heart wanting to go cold again because I wanted that special relationship from him; I felt there was so much we could learn from each other mentally, emotionally, physically, sexually, all the things that make for a strong relationship. This only made me go cold again not by me ignoring him but me turning into a narcissistic playboy but not before dealing with a rough patch of depression.

Shortly after Maxi left to go back home to Germany, things at my workplace took a turn for the worst. That subtle hate was sinking in; there was envy because of how popular I was and the lofty goals I had at wanting to be a Brand Ambassador. I found it fascinating that no one even knew that position existed until I explained that was my ultimate goal within The Big Sports Corporation. Little did I know that my direct managers out of Louisville were out to sabotage me. They purposefully complained about my work as if I was doing something horribly wrong, criticized my management skills, and were talking about me behind my back, which I had my own crafty ways of knowing and finding out this as a fact! To make matters even worse, a co-worker came to me and told me that she was in my direct manager's office and happened to read an email where a Brand Ambassador recruiter had emailed him in regards to me and she saw my manager's response where he suggested they pursue other candidates. Meanwhile, he was bending over backward to help another straight White guy who became interested in the Brand Ambassador position after I had mentioned it, to all the connections he had. I really knew I had to leave when it came to our annual performance ratings, and this man gave me the lowest rating possible. The rating was so low that I was not even eligible to apply for the Brand Ambassador position. It was at this moment I realized how another human being could snap and kill another person. However, I knew my track record was documented and I fought back. I reached out to corporate HR and explained the entire situation and gave them a track record of my accomplishments over the year and my accomplishments with The Big Sports Corporation as a company over my entire career and showcased how the rating he gave me made no sense at all. They looked into the matter and everything got overturned, but the damage was done. I had that blank stare feeling again. Thinking about why did I have to go through that? What did

I do? It hurt and I knew I needed to leave. My last few months at The Big Sports Corporation I was borderline a mute, I hated going to work, I was depressed, and was in a terrible space. I had a talk with my best friend Ava, and she told me she could help me get a job at another Cellular Corporation making double the money and most likely more because she just knew I'd be good at it. I told her to make it happen and she did. When I found out I got the gig at the Cellular Corporation, I gave them a one-month notice and made my way back to Nashville.

CHAPTER 9. ME AND MY WHITE BOYS

When I got back to Nashville, my main focus was just learning my new job and that's what I did for six months. Once I was familiar with everything and knew what I was doing and started making some money, that narcissistic playboy in me I mentioned earlier was ready to run through the city. So far, I have been very vague with my sexual encounters, but I think it's an important thing to understand about me, because I've had multiple conversations with myself trying to figure out why I am the way I am. All the guys I have mentioned in regards to relationships and hook-ups were all White. I have a very strong attraction to White men. When I think about my childhood and how I was bullied, it was always the Black kids. I explained how the Black men would look at me with contempt when they realized I was queer and how the majority of them were drunk, poor, or on drugs and hearing some of the mean things they would say about gay people, and lastly how my dad never seemed to really ever take me under his arm as his son and became just that—drunk, poor, and on drugs. I feel it was a combination of all that, that made me block ever considering wanting to be with a Black man and a subtle form of self-hate; it was off limits for me. On the other hand, when it came to my interactions with White men, it was something so taboo about it, it was taboo. I'm a Black gay man who has an obsession with White men. Strange, I know. Odd, I know. Confusing, I know. I'd go on to explore my infatuation with White men from a variety of angles. Was it because I was brainwashed by a White supremacy society? Maybe. Or could it just be possible that opposites attract? Maybe. Or it could have been that I was traumatized by seeing that porn as a kid and really focusing on that White man's penis. It's a lot to take in. I also dug a little deeper and read about the history of buck breaking back in the slavery days, and it's something that plagues me wondering if I was in some form cursed by that torture. I find it fascinating to hear the viewpoint of others when it comes to interracial relationships, and I've come to realize that there are bits and pieces of truth to a lot of opinions and also some ridiculous opinions when I hear people stating something as fact. However, I've learned that when it comes to connecting with someone, it doesn't matter what they look like, and that my attraction to White men was nothing I needed to shame myself over.

Gabe Powers was a wonderful guy, but when he said I needed to live more, I marinated on that when I became this sniper playboy and I also took the fact that Maxi Milian couldn't commit to me as a grudge to be a player. There was also this toxic mix of all the White boys from when me and Luke used to hit the bars that I watched like a hawk and observe every detail of their interactions to know that I was simply a fetish to them and them thinking, "What is it so special about me that Luke wants to be my best friend?" Clearly, they were a fetish to me as well. It was so interesting being back in Nashville and seeing some of those guys make moves on me, but the thing about it was I didn't want them; as far as I was concerned, they were the equivalent of all the White men who had done me wrong in the past as far as school, work, and any other White person who cursed me with that historical hate; they were scum. I wanted the White men they lusted for and I got them. During this time, the dating app Grindr was all the rage, and I created a profile there that would give me access to some unique White men who would probably never want anyone to know they slept with a Black man. Here are some of my favorite stories.

THE INTERIOR DESIGNER

The app Grindr has always been sort of a creep fest, but I had a full profile that clearly showed my face and muscle-bound body. It was like fish bait. I saw I had a message from a blank profile, and when I clicked on it, it was a picture from an extremely attractive mature gentleman. We texted for a bit and it was a good chat. We discussed what interested us sexually, and he was an open book just like me, and he wanted to meet. He invited me to his place, and on my way there, it was like driving to batman's house—a lot of trees hiding these mansion-like houses, and his place was on this giant hill that overlooked the city. I just remember pulling up thinking, damn. He was at the door waiting for me and greeted me with a kiss; he had asked me the day before what I liked to drink and I told him St. Germain, and he had a glass of it waiting for me in the living room. We sat and talked for about thirty minutes. During that time, he disclosed to me that he was married to another man and that they had an open relationship because his partner was a bit older than he was and couldn't always please him sexually; he also explained to me that he was madly in love with his husband, and there was no other person in the world that he would want to be with. I took that as a sign not to catch feelings. But that was nothing he needed to worry about. After we spoke, he took me on a tour throughout his house. It was stunning. It was beautiful. He actually had magazines with his house on the cover; he explained to me how he was an interior designer and was very appreciative of my compliments. He was a gentleman. We made our way downstairs and it was clear this was the room we were going to fuck. He was a great kisser. Very passionate. Even though he was slightly older than me, he was in great shape, and when we got naked, he just admired my body and I admired him. He was my kind of freak. No holds barred. I just remember fucking him and being inside of him and him knowing when I was about to cum and he pulled me in deeper and said "don't you pull out of me." I just remember *thinking I wish your husband could see us now*, and I came deep inside him. He wanted and loved every drop; I knew this because afterward he said, "Now I get to carry you with me wherever I go." These moments always took me somewhere deep and dark. I'd wonder how many other White men want this man? How many White women want this man? I'd think about all the times I was done wrong by White men and wishing they could be there to watch. I was heartless, and the sex was simply a euphoric drug for me. It also made me think about that connection of sharing your seed because it was so funny every time I'd think of wanting to fuck him again, he'd message; it was like we were connected, and my friend Ava would always be around too because I'd always tell her how great the sex was and that I was craving him, and sure enough, he'd message, and we would always laugh and look in amazement at the coincidence… Crazy, right?

THE SINGER

I met the singer off Grindr as well. It was another blank profile with a message. When I opened it, I just thought it was a fake profile. He was beautiful. Model type. I asked him to send more pictures and he did. I could tell by the selfie pictures and how he texted me that he was real and the fact that he was open to meeting me at Centennial Park. I remember getting to the park and he was just sitting on the steps and, yep, he was real. He looked just like his pictures. Model type. We went for a walk around the park and just talked. He told me he was a singer, but he downplayed it like he was some struggling artist. I came to find out later that was a big lie. Anyway, he wanted to go back to my place, so we did. I remember getting back to my room, and I couldn't stop talking. I wasn't sure he wanted to do anything sexually, but he was just staring at me as if to say, "Are you going to come and get this???" I went and sat close beside him and he put his hand on my leg and I asked him if he was a good kisser. He just started to kiss me; he was all over me; he started taking off his clothes and he said, "I thought you were never going to make a move." He was very sexy, and he knew it. I was actually somewhat intimidated by it, but I also realized he wanted me just as bad as I wanted him. He was a playful hook up, the type you kiss and then push, grab each other real tight and wrestle a bit, stroking each other, dry humping, it was hot. I got off first and then he did. I've never seen someone cum so much in my life; he shot it on my chest, and I just remember thinking, damn, he's basically pissing cum. It was a lot. But I thought it was hot. After we got cleaned up, he left and I did a search and found out he was somewhat of a celebrity. He was a top contestant on one of those music shows. I also found out he wasn't out. I would look at his pictures on the Internet and I could see the pain in his eyes even when he smiled, keeping this secret in. It's probably why he sings so good, I thought. He was truly singing his heart out. Every now and then, I felt bad for him.

THE INTERIOR DESIGNER #2

Grindr had started to become a nuisance. People were messaging me and were basically stalking me. Saying shit like, "I saw you at the gas station," "You walked past me, you can't say hi?" "I'm looking at you right now." So I started creating fake profiles. Once I got a message on one of the fake profiles I had from a blank profile, and I was able to get enough information to find him on Instagram. I used my real profile on Instagram to follow him, and he followed me back. I went through his entire profile and liked a lot of his pictures, and he went through a few of mine and did the same. I didn't want to make that first move to say hello and he didn't either; about six months went by with us just passively interacting with each other through Instagram. I took a trip to Chicago with a friend, and we went out to Boystown, and when we were walking up to one of the bars, he happened to be walking out; we both just looked at each other in shock. It was like we both had just seen a ghost. We just greeted each other and said that it was finally nice to meet. He said he was headed to another bar, and we exchanged numbers, and I told him maybe we could meet up later at another bar and he was game. I couldn't believe I had just seen him. He looked just like his pictures. He was another one I had did a deep dive on. I found out he was once voted one of Nashville's most beautiful people, and he was an interior designer. These damn interior designers. And yes, he knew the previous one I mentioned earlier. I was eager to meet up with him so I messaged him and told him we were headed to Scarlett, which was my favorite bar in Chicago; they play great music and I wanted to dance with him. He got there right when we did, and I bought everyone drinks. He just stood on the wall and stared at me. I kept waving for him to come dance with me, but he'd just shake his head no, and stare. I was all too familiar with this stare. It was the same stare I'd give to a sexy White boy who I was attracted to; I knew he wanted to get me naked. My friend ended up leaving with another group of guys, so I asked him if he wanted to get out of there and go somewhere else; he said we could go back to his hotel. I just looked at him and said, "Okay." This was a classic movie scene, getting back to the hotel, ripping each other's clothes off, and having a flat-out drunk fuck. That next morning, I got up while he was still asleep and showered and had breakfast at his hotel and then went back to mine. I messaged him and told him I was on prep and that he didn't need to worry about me having anything because I get tested on a regular basis and he replied back the same. He also said that he wanted to see me again when we got back to Nashville. About a month went by before I ended up seeing him again, but this time it was different. Everything was planned. I got to his place, and he had some Miguel playing, candles lit, and he was just laying on the couch butt naked. I'd take off my clothes, make my way over to him, and give a good firm grip on his big toe and I'd caress every inch of his body; he was mine, and I'd fuck him like he was mine; he'd whisper in my ear he was mine. Our sex was amazing. He messaged me one day and said that we can no longer meet because he wanted to focus on his relationship. I remember going through his pictures and seeing this one guy in a few of his pictures, but I didn't realize they were still together. I remember thinking this dude ain't shit and he'll be back. And he came back. The sex was too good. He pulled that same shit two more times saying that we couldn't meet again, but at that point, I knew it was too late. I'd came in him so many times that I'm almost sure that my DNA controls a part of him. As I write these words, I'm still fucking him to this day, and he swears he's done with his ex, but if he ever reads this book, he'll know I'm talking about him, and this will be the push he needs to break away from me. I don't like to be mind fucked. At some point, I had the idea in my mind that I liked this guy, but I also realized the sheer fetish I am for him as he is to me. I knew that all I was to him was this hard-dicked Black man who fucks him how he likes to get fucked. I knew that I could never be more than that for him and how it could never be known that him, this uber successful, extremely attractive, White man, was with a Black man. His feelings are artificial. All my experiences with Luke and from the two genuine White men who actually showed me some form of love will always alert my gut feelings to recognize when I'm dealing with a fuck boy.

CHAPTER 10. GAY BLACK MEN

Apparently, Black men being attracted to White men is not a rarity. Luke was getting really serious with his relationship and was still living out of town with his boyfriend, but he visited Nashville from time to time. There was one night when he was in town, and we went out for a drink and a tall Black gentleman who I recognized from my days of playing on the AAU circuit sent us a round of drinks. I already knew he wanted Luke, but when we went over to thank him for the drinks, he tried to play it off by saying he thought we both looked like some interesting people to get to know. He also recognized me, and we connected on how we recognized each other. He played for a top-tier AAU basketball team and was a former D1 player. His name was Jamal. Jamal was extremely intelligent, strategic, and a sucker for White boys too. Once he found out the details about Luke and that he was off limits, he connected more with me around basketball. He invited me out to a league he was playing in and I told him I'd come play. That next week when I went to go play in the league game with Jamal, we balled out!

We had an instant chemistry. It always made me happy knowing that we were both gay out here whooping these straight men's asses on the basketball court. After the game, me and Jamal talked in the parking lot for four hours! We talked about everything—Our families, coming out, music, our outlook on life, where we wanted to be in the future, being Black, being gay, being Black gay men, and our attraction to White men. But to be completely honest, I was ecstatic that he was gay and could ball! He was shocked that I wasn't best friends with Ali, the superstar basketball player from my high school who was also gay. Jamal was the catalyst for bringing that whole friendship together. We all eventually signed up to play for a traveling NGBA team, National Gay Basketball Association and they became my brothers. Me and Luke were like brothers, but with them, it was different, they were Black. There are some things that you can't explain, and I knew those feelings were something they understood being Black gay men. And they could hoop. Especially Ali. I loved the bond that we had because we truly understood each other. The Black gay community is very interesting. You have the ones who are extremely feminine. You have the ones who are DL who will go to the grave with their secret. You have the ones who only want another Black man and hate the fact to see another Black man give a White man the time of day. You have the ones who like White men and act like they can't even talk to another Black man when they are with them. Then you had us, we all had the ability to fit in anywhere and was able to navigate any crowd; it was something that we recognized among each other and where one of us might had a problem. I'd love how we would always have deep discussions on why something just happened and helped each other with a solution.

Jamal and Ali would always make fun of me and say that I was going to marry Luke, but I'd always tell them Luke is my brother, and he has his future husband. I also found it fascinating how Jamal and Ali would fall head over heels for the White boys. I knew we all liked them, but I never thought it would be the thing that would ruin our friendship. Jamal had met this very cute young White kid and swore up and down he was the one. Ali and I would always laugh about Jamal's relationships because every guy he dated was always "the one," but he really wanted to be serious this time. Jamal's new boyfriend's name was Jett. Jamal introduced us to Jett, and I could tell by how Jett would look at me that he was attracted to me. Ali recognized it too and would even call it out from time to time because Jett started to be at all our hangouts, basketball games, and any other event. I didn't think anything of it. I didn't want Jett as I knew he was Jamal's boy. As the time passed, Jamal and Jett started to have some ups and downs in their relationship. Me and Jamal would talk about it, and Jamal was willing to do anything to make that relationship work. There was one time they met me at my gym just to chat for a bit, and I was all pumped after my workout and Jamal started kidding with me saying I was looking all sweaty and sexy; and he threw out the offer for me to hook up with Jett. He said it very casually but in a way that he meant it… He said, "Randolph, how would you feel about hooking up with Jett? It's cool if you want too, I wouldn't mind, let me know. I don't mind sharing. I looked at Jett and he just had a look on his face like, "say yes." Like I said before, I didn't want Jett and that moment for me was just awkward. This is important to understand because a few months went by and Jamal's and Jett's relationship hit a rock and a hard place. Jett knew how close I was to Jamal, and he called me one day and asked to meet with me to talk about everything. We met up and we had a long talk about Jamal and I broke down to Jett, exactly who Jamal is and what he was wanting from him. It was clear to me that Jett was not on the maturity level of Jamal and didn't want to be forced to be molded to a certain person to fit Jamal's image. Jett wanted to be Jett. I understood both points of views and ultimately told him to clearly communicate to Jamal and that they would be fine. Jett stayed almost an hour away and had asked if he could spend the night at my place, and I told him he could sleep on the couch. In the middle of the night, Jett came into my room and got in the bed with me and pulled down my boxers and started to suck my dick; he eventually got on top of me and tried to slide it in and I stopped it. I told him to stop. He got off of me and we went to sleep. The next morning, he apologized to me and asked me not to tell Jamal. I told him I wouldn't. Jamal's and Jett's relationship continued to go downhill, and one day, Jamal called me. Jamal had a way of knowing when something was wrong with me and he asked me if something happened between me and Jett. I told him what happened. Jamal let me know he was hurt and upset by it, but that everything was okay; but it wasn't. A couple of weeks had passed, and I called Jamal to talk and I was mid conversation, and Jamal interrupted me and told me that he was not over what happened between me and Jett. I went on to apologize for what happened. I was sorry I met up with him. I was sorry that it got as far as it did in my bed. I was sorry that I didn't tell Jamal asap. And I apologized for all of it. But that wasn't enough. Jamal and Ali stopped communicating with me. I never thought our friendship would be ruined by something like this. If that situation would have happened with Gabe Powers or Maxi Milian to Jamal or Ali, I would have never given up our friendship for either one of them. I also would have never offered Gabe or Maxi like some prostitute either. It became clear to me who they were and how I was different from them. Yes, we all had an attraction to White men, but they truly put them on a pedestal. Luke had told me they were not to be trusted and that he felt they kept me close to get to him, and I had those thoughts early on; however, they had changed. I also just took that as Luke being jealous of how tight our friendship had become, but Luke might have been right. I found it interesting how they continued to try to remain in close contact with Luke knowing damn well they were not speaking to me, and the whole time Luke would immediately reach back out to me and tell me. I eventually told Luke, "You know they are not talking to me, right?" Luke would say, "Good! Now I can ignore those bitches, I only was cool with them because you were." I also gained access to Maxi Milian's social media account and I saw where Ali had sent dick pics to him. Ali knew Maxi was special to me, I wasn't even mad, besides Maxi rejected his offer. It still saddens me to this day seeing how they became that type of gay Black man, and by that, I mean it was clear to me they were willing to put their gayness first, their deep attraction, their fetish, their loyalty, throw away friendship and family to always please a White man. I would never do that as a Black gay man.

CHAPTER 11. THE MOST HATED

I mourn the loss of Jamal's and Ali's friendship every day because I thought our friendship was so much stronger than that; I thought it was a brotherhood. I used to want to reconcile what we had and hope everything could go back to normal, but I'm afraid that it might be too late. I don't think things could ever go back to what they were. I actually ran into Ali not too long ago, and he acted like nothing ever happened and proceeded to tell me that he and Jamal were currently not on talking terms and the reason was eerily similar to what caused our fall out. Karma's a bitch. I kept it cordial and listened, hung around for a bit, and met his new group of friends and kept it moving. I'll always show them respect because I do respect them, but I know it's best to let go.

Luke went on to marry his lover boy as expected, and as I mentioned before I couldn't have been happier for him. We had a blast at his wedding, and it was very reminiscent of how we used to tear the dance floors up back when we were jumping all over the country; as a matter of fact, he actually tore his wedding pants from dancing so hard. Me and Luke touch base every other week, but he has recently sparked concerns when we do have a chance to see each other in person. He fell into telling these off-kilter race jokes that I just don't think are funny, and it often causes an awkward scene for the other people who are around, as they always get quiet and I will too. I'll just look at Luke with a blank stare and not say anything and carry on with whatever is the topic at hand. I just take this as his new form of wanting some type of attention, kind of like how he used to do back when we were in college. The thing is I know Luke sees me as his brother because even though we have moved on in our lives and don't see each other that often, when I have a chance to meet his new friends, they are always so excited to meet me; they tell me all the great things that Luke has said about me and that he loves me, and it's not just his friends but his actual family too—his dad, his real brother, and all the baseball boys who are basically his brothers who he still spends a lot of time with. Ultimately, I just look at it as he wants to step back to those moments where we were just so young, wild, and free being our crazy selves. I also think it's important to note that the few times Luke has seen me being disrespected, he comes in quick ready to beat somebody's ass, only person I've seen just as quick is my sister. That always meant a lot to me, but he always comes back full circle and expresses to me how he wants me to settle down and that I need to find somebody, but I'm in no rush for that because I'll know when the right person comes along. In the meantime, I truly enjoy my solitude and the options it affords me.

I try to focus on healing my past. I have forgiven my father and have accepted the fact that he has chosen a life of drugs over his family and does not want the help to kick the habit. I'm okay with that. He can call me anytime, and I'll send him the money. My sister hates that I do that, but if that makes him happy, then so be it. I sometimes think of going to save him, but he once tried to set me up. I felt it in my soul that day because he kept insisting I need to meet his "friend" before I left and that I needed to take him to these apartments; when we got there, I saw someone quickly looking out the window and it was extremely odd and my gut was telling me to leave. I've learned how to truly listen to my inner voice as I've gotten older. He was acting all nervous and panicky, and I just told him that I needed to get back on the road to Nashville and I left. He called me a couple of months later, and he would go on to apologize to me about that moment telling me that he almost made a big mistake that day. He knew he was setting me up for something. I never told my mother about this because I felt like she would have driven down there and finished the job of killing him like she wanted to back when she went on that wild man chase. I still love him, but in a way, he is already dead to me.

I think its funny family members will call my mama and ask her if I'm gay. I also notice their behavior when I go to different family events. It's like they want to ask me stuff but don't know how to and then it's the ones who know and don't care and just want to have fun! That's how it should be.

When I came out, I told a good high school friend of mine who is a White straight male, and he replied, "Damn, you got it really bad. You're Black and you're gay. You're like the most hated person on this planet." We both laughed and I looked at him and told him, "I know." I always tell people the truth hurts, but you can't be afraid of it. Trauma and being misunderstood throughout my lifetime are something that have impacted a lot of my relationships. I've since realized how each one of those environments have shaped me into the person I am today. My coworkers used to literally roll on the floor laughing when I would say that infamous line from the movie *Don't Be a Menace to Society While Drinking Your Juice in the Hood*… The line went, "I'm just trying to do to the White man what he has been doing to us for 400 years…What's that? Fuck'em!" In a way, it did become a game to me snatching up and sleeping with every type of White boy you can think of. I'd always give a sinister grin when they would tell me, "You're the first Black guy I've been with." I took pride in ghosting the ones who wanted more and tried to show feelings when all I wanted was to get off and could care less about their feelings. It's an unhealthy habit that I'm working on day to day, fueled by revenge, curiosity, rebellion, and lust.

These days I brainwash myself with a variety of influential Black men. I love listening to Dr. Boyce Watkins because he does a great job of breaking down the urgent crisis that faces Black America and challenges people to think critically. I was devastated by the loss of Kobe Bryant as I loved how he used the hate he received throughout his entire career to constantly elevate to greatness. Reggie Middleton is a brilliant financial guru who amazes me every time I hear him speak. Yet he goes unnoticed and constantly has his information plagiarized and was a victim of a hate crime by the police, which he barely survived. I love Eddie Murphy because his imagery has always lived with me since I was a kid on how he would strategically put Black people in positions of power in all the movies he wrote and directed, and as I've grown older, I've appreciated it that much more. And James Baldwin his work is just priceless.

I recently came across a German couple who have been living in the United States for three years, and they told me they were in the process of moving back to Germany. I asked them why. They told me that there is too much hate in America. I just smiled and said I know.

I get hate from everybody—Black, White, Asian, Mexican, gay, straight, young, old, it doesn't matter. I've learned how to recognize it and make decisions on how I want to learn from the situation or simply walk away. I often go out to the basketball courts and get lost in shooting and manifest all the great things I want out of life; and reminisce on all the hate I've been able to conquer by learning how to think for myself, wanting more for myself and loving myself.